Triple No. 10

Jayne Marek
Bethany Reid
George J. Farrah

The Ravenna Triple Series

*Chapbooks as they were meant to be read—
in good company.*

ISBN: 978-1-7351131-6-6

Published by Ravenna Press
USA
ravennapress.com

FIRST EDITION

Acknowledgments & Biographies

Jayne Marek

Solitary Two-Step

Contents

Mid-Dark

In mid-dark, when chill takes over
this house, my husband lifts blankets
and sits up at the edge
of our bed. I can see
only his bare outline in gray
glimmer that says the moon's
just sunk behind firs, letting go

of this side of earth. I feel
how the weight of his body,
upright, changes the bed's
landform, as if he is lifting away
from me—as he will,
one day, whether he or I
go first, following the silver trail

of moon passing—the way we'll
have to let go, the heft
of our lives lessening but not yet
gone, anchoring half the bed
for a last moment before
he stands and tiptoes toward
the doorway to a room we know is there.

Slip of Light

Morning reflections change when summer sun
enters a window over the kitchen counter
and touches an opposite cupboard, traces

the edge of its door. Time has passed,
the old man thinks, standing at the sink edge
in a faded robe. Crumbs fray

the edges of last night's dishes.   *She* would
have turned to watch the shapes of sun sway
from a coffee cup raised. Would have lifted
    her eyes

to his, met and held them, a double light,
the kitchen cleaner then, but now, forgotten
in the blindness of his grip.

The House of the Lonely Man

The house of the lonely man
at night shows lights on
in two rooms so he can sit in
the living room and stare through
the door to the next where the lamp
shines against a small uncurtained
window, reflecting, as if that single
glow were twice its size. He could
stand up slowly from the flattened sofa
and walk carefully into that other room,
as if about to speak to someone who
won't care if the man pauses to put down
a bottle, and if he stops, perplexed, once
    past
the doorframe, he could turn around
and perceive, over his shoulder, the room
he just left, soft with luminance that
    needs no words
and seems never to have had them.

Neighborhood Conflagrations

How many happen at night, when sirens
rouse sleepers down the block
to peer murky-eyed between bedroom blinds
and see the yellow and red leaping?

How many of us say the same things,
exclamations bursting from our mouths
as our sight clears in a flash, while raging light
falls past us into the dark safe room?

Quickly—how quickly—we think a wish
into merciless space that is now consuming
things we used to know, even the wish itself,
hollow and flying to tatters amid the smoke.

Andalucia

I traveled back to pink sky

when I knelt amid unbelieving
rabbits, starved, in gardens without drink.

Rabbits' eyes shone, angry with the gods
who made this hillside, scraped it

down, then built pink streets,

pink bricks, stucco with its trowel marks,
walls lining the unclosed burrow of my heart.

Spilled wine the color of cobblestones fallen
from those mountains. Everything

dried, accepted this punishment. I went back,
touched hot ironwork twisted like eyelashes

against sand in the wind. Against
the red eye, high overhead,

the mind of the other.

Fire

Here is where we find the most fire:
under our own feet. Amazing
that we can stand amid our lies
and not blink as the clothing on our backs
goes up in an orange blast,
hair wafting out like Medusa's snakes
with white sparks at the snouts,
a hellish halo of pretense.
But who says we are cleansed
by this? Funny, how people we think
will be stonestruck by a falsehood
are still able to walk away, shaking
their heads, brushing the ash
from their hands.

Alarm

A brown alarm clock that stopped twice in a row
        at the same hour
surely had something wrong
        with the mechanism.

It had been your grandmother's, had sat
        in her bedroom all those years
she kept separate from your grandfather,
        with farm dust sifting

through rickety window frames and doors
        left ajar to catch
any movement of the August air, laden
        with scents of manure.

The clock was round and big as a grapefruit,
        a fruit she never saw
until she was in her fifties. Limitations,
        that's what people lived with

in the country back in those days, far from
        the general stores
she carried her coins to now and then.
        In winter's deep nighttimes

she could watch the clock's radium hands
        and numbers glow
for slow hours, marveling at the science of it,
        the clock face

turned to her, unlike her husband's.
        And the clock
stayed on its shelf, never flew across the room
        to strike her.

She may have thought about the young women
        decorating
the clock dials not far away, in small-town
        Ottawa, Illinois,

women with jobs that got them out
        of their houses, offered a wage.
In later years, she heard how those workers
        fell ill, their jaws

turned porous, grotesque sores on their lips
        from licking
the brushes to sharpen them,
        to more precisely paint

the curves of the numerals of time.
        When she turned eighty,

you took your grandmother out to see
        the beautiful angels

in the Ottawa cemetery, floating above
        the green hills
in mist from the river. How cool
        they must have seemed,

the smooth lawns under trees, the pale
        marble headstones
of angels lifting ribbons, their hair flowing,
        gowns so clean.

Looking for the Roundhouse

at the end of the street in what is now
and probably was always a poorer part of town,
past battered cars parked crookedly,
houses not painted for half a century,
broken tree trunks as tall as a person,
evidence of the hard hand of life
that struck here more often than elsewhere
where my mother grew up

in the Depression with six siblings and a thin
mother of her own distracted by the heat
that cooked this airless block in Illinois summer,
when I returned curious about the railroad
that used to tie this country together—
only remnants now such as the spur tracks
and the roundhouse I had seen on a map
at the musty museum—

I followed the heaved-up sidewalk toward
impenetrable brushline that had grown up
along the track bed and even though I knew
children and wanderers would have found a way
through, I could not see it, and then an old man

in too-big overalls appeared at my elbow
immediately as happens in country areas
asking what I was looking for

his posture a question mark;
wasn't there a roundhouse for the trains back here
I said and he thought about it but said he
had not lived on this street then
but yes the train tracks, everybody knew those,
although a stranger alone probably wouldn't
go looking in there, and then he watched me—
what else could he do to tell
about how money and jobs chugged away
years ago and never returned

so that the town settled deeply into dust,
the roots and weedy growths,
the people who watched rails submerge
in grass and the sidewalks fracture
like friends and family and time—
things that come will go, whispered the crickets
and the man and I nodded together quietly;
I said goodbye and he watched
amicably as I walked off under intense sun
that could not open the tangle of leaves
at the end of the street

Direct Feed

Enter the dust of memory that lies
against splintered walls and fences
at the Stephenson County Fair, rural Illinois,

1961. Because it wasn't our first
time there, we knew where to go for corn,
popping fat buttered kernels

in our mouths, and beehives of cotton candy
that stuck to our cheeks all day, dirtying.
Always a manure smell, babbles of sheep

and hens, Holsteins in pens, mourning their fields.
Rides and games cost a quarter apiece,
so mostly we walked: exhibit halls,

canvas pavilions that smelled like the Army
in August heat. Enter one building featuring
a new thing: a camera set overhead at the entrance,

sending live action to a television screen
as we walked in. *Look!* Mom gestured,
and out of habit I flinched

so hard it hurt, as if I'd been struck
after all. *What's wrong with you?*
Mom demanded, and said

it embarrassed her that *everyone could see*
my instant recoil. Not her raised arm
that I'd learned to duck, but the television eye

that played out our secret's beast truth.

Unfolded

In leafy handwriting I have not forgotten
his words look thin and young, as we were then,
basswood saplings stirring
in a breeze, their tresses filled with sparrows.

These old letters found again,
frail, and with frayed folds—how close they have
    come
to being discarded—simmer with heat from
those summers we drove endless gravel roads,

dusted with sepia, figures in tinted photographs.

Today the follies in this handful
of letters strike me as melancholy. I bend,
gathering the weakness of years between difficult
    fingers,
finding in this box of papers our days

spelled out more bare and plain than I hoped
they would be. As I read, the words constrict—
a buzz near my ears, a bee that circles in wait
for the opening of green buds

that it will never sip.

Tidal

Fishing boats add silver tails
    this morning, the only certain
        lines through fog. As
you think how last year
    brought its near-drowning
        tides, more of the ocean inlet
takes shape; lances of fir
    crowns cut
        clouds that the mundane
landforms cannot,
at least so early

in the day, another with low-
    lying overcast. Waiting
        was unfamiliar before
you found this window
    in your own home
        where a hand of eternity
presses, its transparent
    palm wide
        to catch or release.

Set Out to Grow

This morning, I opened curtains and saw the
    beheaded
squash plant that was about to set fruit
holding up one wan finger in its pot.
On two previous days, the plastic birdbath lay
on its open face, astonished. I suspect the return

of the fawn that in mid-July had slinked into
the yard, its ribs bold with shadows.
For most of a week, it browsed
the gorgeous blossoms, itself bright-eyed
if skinny unto death. Not all of them survive.

You name it, coyotes, stray dogs, even
the eagles that we are blasé about
or a raccoon with nothing on its mind
would take down a fawn for sport.

Alone, the young deer shredded
tips of flowers; leaves holed by slugs
lost their edges too; methodically the fawn
mowed all the violets. I saw it later
reclined on cedar chips, its sides heaving.

One day, no fawn. August scattered pine pollen
on the sad discount squash start I had put
in a too-large pot, an extravagance of soil.
It took weeks to raise four flat leaves
and set one yellow flower.

This morning, the squash stub, and the young
     deer,
unspotted now, sleek and rounded,
is working its way among dandelions gone to seed,
leaving stems slight but sharp as promises.

Leaf-Washing, Japan

A red-capped crane amid pine trees
steps gently, slim legs flexing like twig-tips,
the tall bird's cap a red disk, a winter sun
against white-snow feathers.

Gently, slim legs flexing like twig-tips,
the tall bird sifts through the leaf-litter,
sun against its white-snow feathers
and green layers of fallen leaves

as the tall bird searches in leaf-litter.
Black neck, black eye fix upon
a single dark-green fallen leaf. The bird
pauses in thought, an arc of attention,

its black neck, black eye fixed upon
that leaf, its lovely harplike shape.
A pause for thought, an act of attention,
then it picks up the leaf delicately,

neck curved like the leaf's harplike shape.
The crane steps toward a pond
and dips in the leaf, twice, delicately,

then pushes the green slip under. It waits

now at the edge of the pond
to watch a ring of ripples stretch
from where the green slip went under, waits
patiently in this placid forest

while rings of silver ripples stretch
wide in gray January light—
then probes for the leaf, gift of the forest,
fishes it from the water, swallows it whole.

This pleasure, in thin January light, comes
from the fresh green of the washed leaf—
fished from water and swallowed whole—
by the red-capped crane amid pine trees.

Ars Poetica

There is the part that loves.

There is a part that listens
to the musical rustle underfoot.

Another part tastes
the stem of a poem, its leaves, its shell,
and finally finds the kernel.

This part happens and happens.
The taster deeply attentive
learns which shapes are fruit or root,
which are softer to consume,

which slide their wet fibers under skin, which
globes and petals imbue fragrance. Even leaves
with spines may release essences at the touch
of rain or sun, a hand that accepts
plantings that sting the hand.

There is the part in earth
for each of these, strewn with bugs' wings,

bird messes, decaying stems. The part
that loves also loves these,

its touch blunt as a worm.
That part that wants everything
sinks into the garden process

of one word after another, taking it in,
exhaling it as sweetness,

what it craved all along.

Bethany Reid

The Thing with Feathers

Contents

Without Breath

Imagine the breath of God –

God moving the origins of water
(suddenly fish, whales,

coral) and your soul
sloshing, oars
thudding against gunwales

God – abated –

the crick of frogs fainter
as you pull from shore.

You Cannot Fold a Flood

> *You cannot fold a Flood –*
> *And put it in a Drawer –*
>   -Emily Dickinson

Taking it up like a tablecloth,
she gives it a shake –

dark eddies unfurl, swirl and silver,
set into flight Teal

and Harlequin ducks, knives and spoons,
pewter dishes, storm gray

clatter of crockery, smash
of glass as the world breaks, her eye

reflected in shards of gravy boat,
sugar bowl, oars dipping

into waves red as sunset, littered
with livestock, fences, bridges –

lightning in her fingertips,
she folds the flood in half

and in half again, lays it
shimmering in its drawer.

Bright, Impossible

Pressing her pencil to the top
of the page, she doesn't know
where this will carry her,

but she unwinds it,
a clew of yarn,
as the poem inches from caterpillar

to chrysalis, its promise
a long time held
back, the middle drooping,

so heavy it threatens
to collapse –
wings not yet imagined,

opening with their
bright, impossible
flare.

What Was She Afraid of?

As a child, nothing –
carried a snake

in her pocket, leapt from a bridge,
arms feathered with sunlight.

Intent as a monk
over an illustrated manuscript,

she studied the carcass of a crow,
its shell of hollow bones

cloaked in wings.
Writing, she was that fearless,

snapped open "afraid"
and unweaved her life from it –

cupping it in her hands,
bringing it to her lips.

But Who Suspects the Waitress of Poetry?

My Life had Stood – a Loaded Gun –
-Emily Dickinson

If you could, you'd go back
and break her from that stale past
where she was twenty

and coffee cost 25 cents.
Where red-winged blackbirds
still sing from the cattails

in the swamp behind the restaurant.
You'd rev your engine
in the parking lot, lean on your car horn.

Seeing you, she'd run outside,
pulling off her apron,
unpinning her hair –

a line from Dickinson trailing
like smoke
from her red lips.

What Flood Does

Flood disorders pond and stream,
insists on ardor

of rushing water, limbs,

mud, the ordure
of carcass. Flood doesn't respect a fence,
turns out the field's pockets,

scours mint and nettle
from creekbanks.

Cause and recourse,

flood pulls down saplings
and giant maples together.
Flood loves a bridge,

loves to caress with its tongue
those high, amorous thighs

as it runs by.

Though She Didn't Consult the Thesaurus

The Props assist the House
Until the House is built
              -Emily Dickinson

For her – reality,
though it wasn't fact,
ledger or nail, left her
no nail to hang her hat on,
had no name like Atlantis
or Neverland, did not skip
like a chimera off
the stage onto what only looked
to be solid ground, climbed
no tilt-a-whirl of fancy,
figment of the fantastic,
vaguest of vagaries,
her every dim notion,
every reverie, every pipe lit
with nightmare, with rainbow
hallucinations, the merest fabrication
of paradise, fairyland, utopias –
all bright delusions,
and what invention
would she wish herself wed to
but this, a surface slippery
as silk, clouds built of
gossamer?

That Drift of Laughter

> *The Soul selects her own Society –*
> *Then – shuts the Door –*
> > -Emily Dickinson

The soul, she thought she knew.
It was slender, selecting.

The drift of laughter
from her room –

> *her own society.*

The heart has to be invited,
though she's a scary friend,

always thumping away
as if the body matters.

Dickinson's heart troubled her,
wanted other bodies,
longed for the ocean (for mermaids),

thought soul – a bore.
No wonder they kept her on a chain.
No wonder she closed the door.

Emily's Wedding

I felt a Funeral, in my Brain –
but it was only the abyss
dressed in white and black,
some fool handing out

bits of fate like cake.
It was Death
dealt out in scraps, all of us
wedded to it from conception,

and dying like flies.
I felt a funeral –
knew union and disunion,
guests lined up,

a gauntlet,
a conductor (his *boots of lead)*
holding up his watch
and thundering,

"Whom God hath joined – "
when it was God Himself
setting us asunder.

Every rite a funeral,

the universe teasing us into
her *freckled bosom.*
One more *funeral* −

in my brain.

When Eden Imagines Emily

Who bridles the octopus
or asks that it submit
to grammar?

Eden's green pool
loved, beloved of Eve –
when she chose,

pool chose too,
holding up its face, a mirror
to impossible longing.

Her Circumference

My Business is Circumference.
                    -Emily Dickinson

No one to be diminished to a single line,
not the white dress, not the gesture
of picking up a pen. She wavers
when you look, the moon reflected
in a pond, spins thought into words,
an orb spider spinning its tapestry
for morning frost. She sits in the halo
of light the lamp casts, a book
of poems, a lexicon, a Bible open
on her lap. The dream is always
what you cannot know, her glance –
away – her glasses folded in her hand.
The horizon closes on hollyhock,
on the magnolia tree, on bush beans
and raspberries. You escape this net
only to flipper back, only to whisper
against her ear. There is no line here
but what the lamp drops to the rag rug,
two circles bounding on one another.

Ignis Fatuus

A savage depression. Not
feeling, but its lack,
what held her spine erect
dropping like a robe.
The heart an empty cage.
If she drinks all the despair,
she'll be drunk on despair.
Is that a light
at the end of the tunnel,
or only *ignis fatuus,*
miasma, fairy light, fool's gold?
She's like coyote
in the old cartoons –
roadrunner always gets away.
Hope's not a bird but the train
about to flatten her.

Emily's Letter from Tunis

Can clarity be as simple
as *cochineal* –

                the hummingbird's rush
and resonance crushed on your sill,

      the knot of its heart untied?

For too long death
has muddled the news.

                Frozen, adamantine.

Beneath a sky of tin,
you read about Dickinson's hummingbird,
imagine her choosing "Tunis"
(her eroticized East),
the letter that never comes –

except the world does write back,
jangling, unlettered,
nothing so clear as a bird,

or your life itself, lifting its head

tiny and blind as any maggot
          into *cochineal* and *emerald,*

such clamor of light.

Hopefully

> *"Hope" is the thing with feathers –*
> -Emily Dickinson

I want a hope with hide,
with squat feet like the Komodo,
its long back swaying
snake-like as I scurry.

Forget feathers. Forget wings.
I won't be flying
any distance. Only
a trudge from A

to B, arriving safe in the
intimidating luggage of my body.
I want all I bear
to make the passage with me.

Her Begging Bowl

Life is over there, she wrote,
setting it on a high shelf.

Rising at night, she'd
light her lamp, take out a scrap

of paper, a pencil stub, her fragile,
fractured life. It had to be set somewhere,

so she arranged it into lines
abutting white space. And what could be

more like life than that?
A newer Sevre pleases,

she wrote, imbuing the fine china
with a longing to be of use

(*You there – I – here –*),
as if it, too, begged to be broken.

Her Short History of Falling

Memory of her mother's footfall
as she crossed the hallway,
the fall of a single breath,
fall in *folly* and in *foal,* fire's spark,
its arc and flash downward,
hems lowered, the trip
over the porch step, leaf-fall and snow-
fall, morning fog, a syllable
dropped at the end of a word,
the Amen at the end of a prayer,
the voice, a whisper,
her hand limp on the bedcover,
the owl's following flight
to the vole's heart, knell of a bell,
lid of the piano closing
on its keys.

Her Waltz in Floodtime

The last big windstorm brought down
our oldest tree,

an early apple, pale and sweet.
This season's flood fills the orchard,

lapping those remaining,
plum and apple and pear.

Rising water takes the woodpile
in its arms. The spirit

of that old tree was Poetry –
how she must have loved that feeling

of being carried away.

Emily in Spring

> *He fumbles at your Soul*
> *As Players at the Keys*
>   -Emily Dickinson

Slick new leaves and sticky blossoms –
birth pangs, wind

tugging treetops,
spattering hail,

the windshield metronome
of wipers,

hands fumbling at the keys –

but what keys – not your music –
one wrong note after another.

Emily's Direction

Find your way back despite the darkness, despite
   Brazil and the Portuguese Fleet. Find your way

eyeless, tongueless, your fingers thickened
   by calluses, the way not coded in hymnals, not

on anyone's list of instructions – no index,
   no table of contents, no concordance. Let your path

be lit by bleak sunsets after communion with tortoises
   on mattresses left in the rain. Carry

an unlit candle, a mildewed photograph,
   a red satin pillow. Walk roads littered with fiddles,

with cello strings and clarinet reeds. Trust
   your two good feet. Trust hummingbirds

amid purple flowers. Trust the barest vibration.
   Let life carry you like a tune.

Like Emily, She Hears a Buzz

Maybe I did hear a fly buzz
but I hadn't died.
I wasn't dressed in white.
I never said, "I do."

So if a fly buzzed, what
stopped me from buzzing, too,
zipping right out that window?

I don't think I was a fly —

I was all in black and gold
like a bee or a queen.
Everyone bowed and buzzed
as I passed by.

George J. Farrah

My Trip North

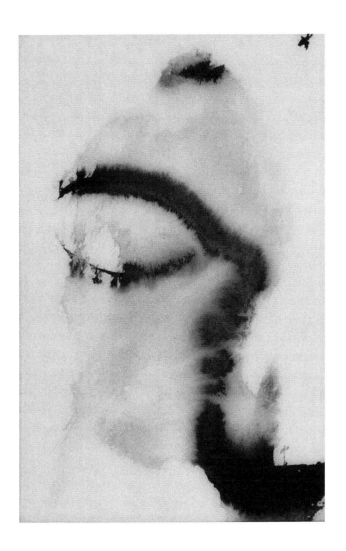

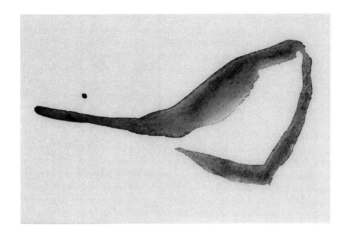

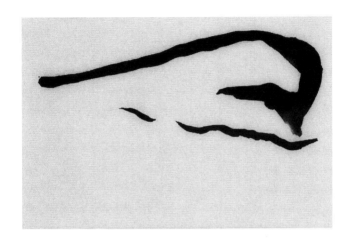

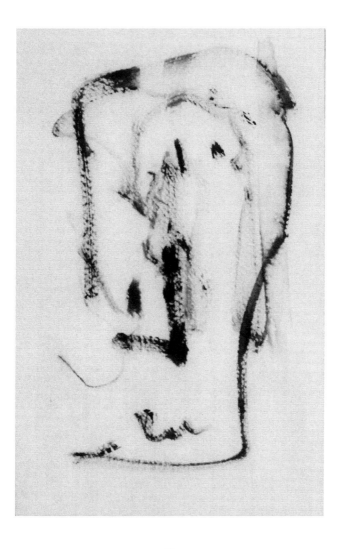

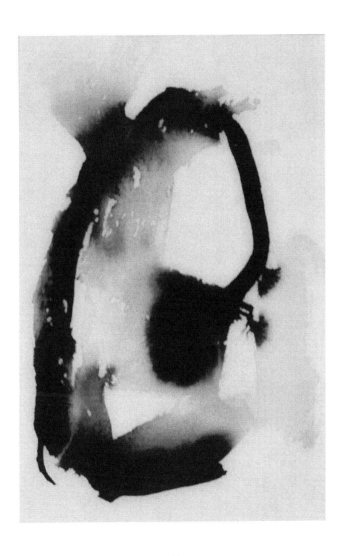

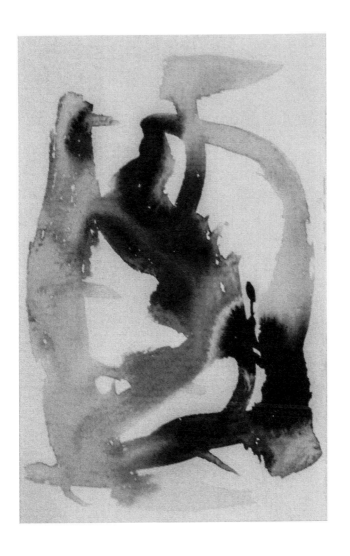

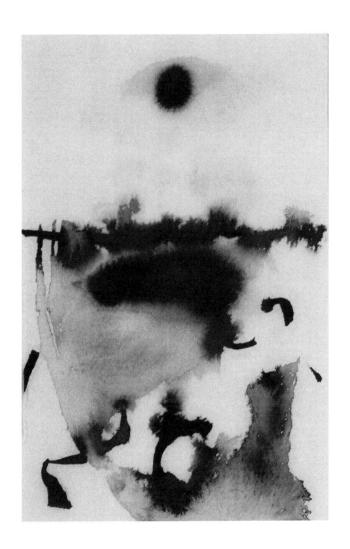

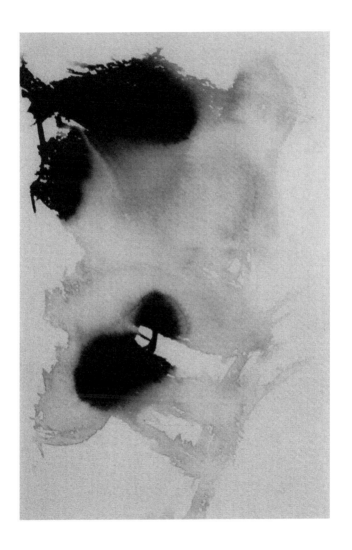

Bethany acknowledges with thanks the prior publication of some of these pieces: *Bird's Thumb 1* 2018, You - Cannot Fold a Flood; *Crosscurrents* 2013, Emily's Wedding, I Heard a Buzz; *Floating Bridge Review 2* 2009, Hopefully; *New Madrid Summer* 2017, Ignis Fatuus.

George J. Farrah holds a Master of Fine Arts Degree from Bard College, The Milton Avery Graduate School of the Arts, Annandale-on-Hudson, New York. He maintains an active exhibition schedule and his paintings are in numerous private and corporate art collections. He is also a poet, with a collection, *The Low Pouring Stars*, and pamphlet, *Insomniac Plum,* from Ravenna Press, a chapbook, *Walking as a Wrinkle* from Moria Press, and *Relieved of Their Whispers,* forthcoming from Ravenna.

Biographies & Acknowledgments

Jayne Marek's books include *In and Out of Rough Water* and *The Tree Surgeon Dreams of Bowling*. Her work appears in *One, Spillway, Calyx, Women's Studies Quarterly, Salamander, Eclectica, Cortland Review, The Lake, Notre Dame Review,* and elsewhere. Winner of the Bill Holm Witness poetry contest, she has received Best of the Net and Pushcart nominations.

The author thanks the editors of the following publications in which some of these poems, or versions thereof, previously appeared: *Bellevue Literary Review,* Set Out to Grow; *The Cortland Review,* Andalucia; *The Curlew* and *Fourth & Sycamore,* Ars Poetica; *Naugatuck River Review,* Alarm; *One,* Unfolded; *River Poets Journal "Windows" Anthology,* Tidal; *The Sea Letter,* The House of the Lonely Man; *Shantih,* Leaf-Washing, Japan; *Stirring: A Literary Collection,* Fire; *Up North Lit,* Direct Feed.

Bethany Reid's two most recent books are *Sparrow,* which won the 2012 Gell Poetry Prize, and *Body My House* (2018). Her poems have won numerous awards, including the Jeanne Lohmann Poetry Prize, *Calyx*'s Lois Cranston Memorial Prize, and *The MacGuffin*'s Poet Hunt Prize. She lives and writes in Edmonds, Washington, and blogs at www.bethanyareid.com.